# THE OFFICIAL ANNUAL 2016
## HIBERNIAN FC

WRITTEN BY DAVID FORSYTH
DESIGNED BY STEPHEN WILLIAMSON

A Grange Publication

©2015. Published by Grange Communications Ltd., Edinburgh, under licence from Hibernian Football Club. Printed in the EU.

Photographs © SNS Group.

ISBN 978-1-910199-47-3

# CONTENTS

# WELCOME TO THE LATEST OFFICIAL HIBERNIAN ANNUAL

What a year it has been. We've seen huge change at your Club, both on the pitch and off it.

On the pitch we've seen our team improve under Head Coach Alan Stubbs and his staff. We are determined to play exciting, attacking football and we have developed a squad of talented young footballers. Our hopes are high that we will get back into Scottish football's top flight.

Off the pitch, we have changed things too. In particular, our share offering is aimed at giving the supporters a real stake in the Club, with the chance to own up to 51% of it. Our first two Supporter Directors were directly elected by season ticket holders and are now fully established as Non-Executives on our Board, ably representing fans at the highest level.

We've seen supporters buy shares directly as individuals and we've also seen the growth of Hibernian Supporters Limited, now a very significant shareholder in its own right. Representing many hundreds of fans who are its members, it will only grow in the months ahead.

Through the Hibernian Community Foundation, we are touching more lives and making an even greater difference to people in our community, through encouraging more active lives, through helping them learn new skills, through helping people find work, and through many other ways.

Under the leadership of Chief Executive Leeann Dempster we continue to focus on improving all the time, and that also includes all the ways in which we talk to, and listen to, our supporters.

We hope you enjoy the season, we hope it has a happy ending for all Hibernian supporters, and we hope you enjoy this year's Annual.

# SEASON REVIEW

## 2014-15

## AUGUST

Hibernian's competitive season kicked off with a Petrofac Training Cup match against Rangers at Ibrox on August 5th, with new Head Coach Alan Stubbs and his staff barely in the door and player recruitment still ongoing as the Club came to terms with its unexpected relegation from the top flight.

A match against the favourites for the Championship away from home was hardly the easiest of openings, but a youthful Hibernian side played their way steadily into the game despite going behind to a goal after 15 minutes, and were soon dictating play with a fluent passing game. An equaliser came, and only a harsh sending off which saw Hibernian down to ten men swung the balance back towards Rangers as the game went into extra time, with Rangers scoring as another Hibernian player suffered a cramp attack.

The tie was lost, but the portents for Hibernian fans were encouraging.

The opening SPFL Championship league match against Livingston at Easter Road a few days later saw Hibernian win 2-1, with goals by El Alagui and – remarkably – goalkeeper Mark Oxley. But the following match at Tynecastle was to prove less happy. A missed penalty, a player red-carded, and a narrow 2-1 defeat to the side who were to take confidence from their win and go on a league-winning run thereafter. A Scottish League Cup win at home to Dumbarton was secured with a 90th minute goal by Sam Stanton. Another Championship loss followed, 0-1 at home to Falkirk, and then a reverse away to Alloa wrapped up an unhappy first month, particularly as striker Farid El Alagui, seen as a key man in the Club's plans, suffered a serious injury.

# SEPTEMBER/ OCTOBER

Before the transfer window slammed shut Congo international Dominique Malonga was brought in to bolster the Club's striking options following the injury suffered by Farid, and was in place for the Club's fixtures in September.

The month kicked off with a scrappy 3-2 win at Easter Road against Cowdenbeath, with another late winner, this time from Jason Cummings. Defeat to a useful Queen of the South side at Recreation Park by a solitary goal was next up. But all the while Head Coach Alan Stubbs had been preaching patience as he worked hard to instil his ideas in his new charges, and the next match was to provide great encouragement with a 2-0 win away in the Scottish League Cup to Premiership side Ross County. Next, a 3-1 Championship win was secured away to Rangers with goals by Cummings (2) and David Gray. The scoreline didn't flatter Hibernian. Next game saw Hibernian batter Raith Rovers yet, remarkably, secure only a 1-1 draw at Easter Road.

Another draw at Easter Road followed as Dumbarton successfully set up for a tie, and the failure to kill teams off was seeing Hibernian lose ground to title rivals Hearts and Rangers. The killer instinct was discovered away to Livingston when Hibernian ran out 4-0 winners, with goals from Malonga, Handling, McGeouch and Heffernan. Next up was the Edinburgh Derby return, at Easter Road, with Hibernian dominating and playing fluently in an exciting 1-1 draw, in which Malonga opened the scoring just before half-time. Hearts looked like suffering defeat, and only secured the point courtesy of a 30-yard 92nd minute strike.

October ended with a thrilling Scottish League Cup quarter final at Easter Road against high-flying Premiership Dundee United. The game was one of the best of the season, with a 3-3 scoreline at the end of extra time seeing the game only decided 7-6 in United's favour on penalties. Both sides were applauded from the pitch at the end of an exhilarating contest. The end of October saw Hibernian fans begin to see a more positive way ahead.

# NOVEMBER/ DECEMBER

The winning form continued, with an away win at Cowdenbeath secured by goals from Hanlon and Cummings. A goalless draw at Easter Road against Queen of the South was followed by a 6-3 whipping of Dumbarton away, with Dominique Malonga securing a hat-trick and the match ball. Hibernian's entry to the William Hill Scottish Cup saw Alloa despatched 2-1 after Hibernian had gone behind in 15 minutes, the goals coming courtesy of Craig and Gray.

Bogey side Falkirk lay in wait in December, and at the Falkirk Stadium another Championship reverse was suffered, Hibernian going down 1-0 in a disappointing affair to an injury time goal. A return to Easter Road the following week saw a comfortable 2-0 win secured against Alloa, Handling and Malonga scoring, and the final fixture before Christmas saw Raith Rovers beaten 3-1 in Kirkcaldy with goals from Cummings, Fontaine and Malonga.

The post- Christmas fixture was to prove a season highlight, Rangers coming to Easter Road to be soundly beaten 4-0 by a rampant Hibernian, with the goals shared between Gray, Cummings, Robertson and Craig. The year had ended on a high.

# JANUARY/
# FEBRUARY

2015 began as 2014 had ended, with a big fixture against a title rival, as Hibernian travelled across the city to meet Hearts. Again Hibernian played fluent football, and took the lead in 23 minutes through Jason Cummings, but Hearts struck back before half-time to level and the match finished 1-1. Hibernian had served notice that on their day, they could match any other side with the quality of their football.

That storming form was taken into the next match, at Easter Road against Falkirk, with Hibernian taking a well-deserved 3-1 lead into the half-time break, with Cummings scoring a brace. The second-half proved less kind, with chances to kill the match missed followed by an own-goal and a frustrating and calamitous few minutes in which Falkirk levelled at 3-3.

The frustration felt at Easter Road was taken out on Cowdenbeath in the following fixture, the Fifers blitzed in a 5-0 defeat that could have been more, with five different players, Hanlon, Cummings, Robertson, Booth and Stevenson.

A difficult away fixture in Dumfries followed against a strongly performing Queen of the South on the artificial pitch at Palmerston. Hibernian played well, and a well-earned 2-0 win was gained with both McGeouch and Robertson scoring. A Martin Boyle goal helped Hibs earn a disappointing 1-1 draw against Raith Rovers at Easter Road.

Arbroath came to Easter Road in early February in the William Hill Scottish Cup, and – playing good football – gave their hosts a genuine scare after taking an early lead. But Hibernian refused to panic, kept playing patient football, and ran out 3-1 winners with second-half goals from Djedje and McGeouch and an own goal.

Another visit to Ibrox followed, and it continued to prove a happy hunting ground. Despite a much more aggressive and positive Rangers performance, Hibernian showed a ruthless streak in winning 2-0 with goals from Robertson and Stevenson, the second, in particular, a contender for goal of the season. Dumbarton were beaten 3-0 at Easter Road, Djedje again scoring and Malonga scoring twice, before the month ended with a 1-0 away win against Alloa.

# MARCH / APRIL

A William Hill Scottish Cup quarter-final at Easter Road saw Hibernian defeat Berwick Rangers 4-0 with the goals coming from Cummings and Stevenson in the first half, and Stanton and Fontaine in the second.

Championship business was resumed with a 2-1 win against Livingston at Easter Road, goals from Cummings and Djedje, followed by goals from Fyvie and Cummings securing a 2-0 win at Cowdenbeath.

The business end of the season was upon us, with Hearts dominating the league it was down to Rangers and Hibernian to contest second spot, with Queen of the South and Falkirk fighting it out for the other play-off spot. So when Rangers came to Easter Road, the match had real edge and under new boss Stuart McCall the Ibrox side edged a hard-fought encounter to secure a morale boosting win. Hibernian suffered another setback away in Kirkcaldy, going down 2-1 to Raith Rovers, and then suffered a third defeat on the bounce at home to Queen of the South.

But the blip was over when Dumbarton were beaten 2-1 away, with the goals from Hanlon and Cummings, and then champions-elect Hearts were beaten 2-0 at Easter Road with goals by Cummings and El Alagui, back from injury. Livingston away was next, and that hurdle was duly cleared with a comfortable 3-1 win with the goals coming via Robertson, Cummings and Malonga. A 4-1 win at home against Alloa again saw the goals spread between four different players, with Cummings and Malonga again amongst them.

One of the season's major disappointments was suffered in April at the hands of Falkirk at Hampden, when Hibernian – despite dominating the match and creating many opportunities – lost the Scottish Cup semi-final by a solitary goal.

# MAY

May was a huge month in Hibernian's calendar. The Championship campaign was to end with an away trip to bogey side Falkirk, with second place still undecided between Hibernian and Rangers.

Hibernian, still smarting from an undeserved Cup semi-final defeat, exacted some measure of revenge with a comprehensive 3-0 win at the Falkirk Stadium, with goals from Boyle, Cummings and Malonga rendering the result of Rangers encounter with Hearts at Tynecastle irrelevant as Hibs finished as runners-up.

That meant a long delay until the winner of the 3rd v 4th play-off was decided between Rangers and Queen of the South. When Rangers came through, Hibernian had another visit to Ibrox to negotiate. In a tense and close affair, Rangers proved more clinical on the day and won 2-0. Despite having several chances, Hibernian were unable to score – a fact that was to come back to haunt the team during the return at Easter Road.

On May 23rd, at Easter Road, Hibernian laid siege to the Rangers goal, dominating the match and creating a number of chances and half chances. A clever goal by Cummings in injury time provided a tiny glimmer of hope, which was extinguished by the referee's whistle. Hibernian fans applauded the team from the pitch despite the failure to progress. Supporters had seen the team develop through the season, and liked what they saw in terms of the exciting football being played, and the talented young players being developed.

# HIBERNIAN
## HISTORICAL TRUST

The Hibernian Historical Trust is a charity established to protect, preserve and promote the history of the Club by collecting and displaying artefacts and memorabilia.

It is an important role, promoting Hibernian's prominent place in the development of the Scottish game and also in reaching out to existing and future fans through its activities, particularly in education. A successful Open Day and tour as part of the Leith Festival was held by the Trust during the summer, with around 3000 visitors to the stadium enjoying the experience.

In addition, several major exhibitions have been mounted in the West Stand, and this year these included outstanding exhibitions on the role played by the Club in the First World War and the 25th anniversary of the Hands Off Hibs campaign which helped save the Club from extinction. If you are interested in learning more about the Trust, or getting involved, visit the website at:

www.hibshistoricaltrust.org.uk

## CONTALMAISON

In 2004 a group of (Hearts) football supporters from Edinburgh were responsible for the raising of a Cairn at Contalmaison in France to commemorate the soldiers of the 15th and 16th battalions of the Royal Scots from Edinburgh, Lothians and Fife who fell at the Battle of the Somme in 1916.

The small village of Contalmaison was the intended objective for the Royal Scots on the first day of battle, a destination that was only briefly held, hundreds dying in the attempt. The battle, which lasted from 1 July until 18 November cost the British army almost 60,000 casualties on the first day alone, 20,000 dead, and is said to be the bloodiest battle in military history.

Each year on the anniversary of the battle a representative from Hibernian has laid a wreath at the Cairn and this summer, along with representatives from Hearts, Raith Rovers, Falkirk and Dunfermline, Tom Wright from the Hibernian Historical Trust laid a wreath on behalf of the club.

During the trip the party also stopped off at the British Military Cemetery at Loos where a wreath was laid on behalf of Hibernian by Tom Wright at the grave of an unknown soldier, one of many in the graveyard. In 1910, almost 100 years after they fell, the bodies of 20 soldiers were discovered during building work, all but one of them unidentified, and last year they were buried in the cemetery with full military honours.

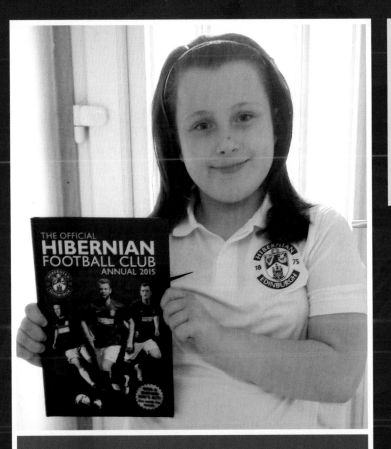

The winner of last year's Kid's Kit Competition was Emma Stafford from Edinburgh and here she is sporting her signed kit. Well done Emma!

# HIBERNIAN MEET & GREET COMPETITION

This year we have an AMAZING prize on offer. One lucky entrant will win a Meet and Greet session at the Hibernian training centre which will include a private tour, meeting the manager and the players, as well as watching the team train. PLUS they will get a whole host of autographs and photos! Wowzers! How good is that?!

Sharpen your pencils and get your thinking caps on. We would like to know in 100 words or less who your all-time favourite Hibernian player is and why.

## PLEASE SEND YOUR ANSWERS:

*By email:*
**frontdesk@grangecommunications.co.uk** with HIBERNIAN FC COMPETITION 2016 in the subject line.

*By post:*
**Hibernian FC Competition 2016, Grange Communications Ltd, 22 Great King Street, Edinburgh, EH3 6QH.**

Please note: Entrants must provide their full name, age, address and a daytime telephone number in order to make a valid entry.

## TERMS AND CONDITIONS
2016 Hibernian FC Competition

### ENTRY

1. Grange Communications Ltd (registered office: 22 Great King Street, Edinburgh, EH3 6QH) is the promoter of the Hibernian FC Annual Competition 2016 ("Competition").

2. By entering the Competition, entrants agree to be bound by these terms and conditions ("Conditions") and confirm that all information submitted is true, accurate and complete. Grange Communications Ltd reserves the right to verify the eligibility of any and all entrants and may, at its sole discretion, disqualify any entrant that fails to satisfy the eligibility requirements. Entrants shall at all times act in good faith towards Grange Communications Ltd.

3. Employees of Grange Communications Ltd or Hibernian FC or any of their associated companies or subsidiaries (and their families) are excluded from entering the Competition.

4. Entry into the Competition is free (except for any standard cost of postage) and on the basis of one entry per person.

5. In order to enter the Competition and to be considered for the prize, entrants must answer the question posed and submit their entries to Grange Communications Ltd either by email to frontdesk@grangecommunications.co.uk with HIBERNIAN FC COMPETITION 2016 in the subject line or by mail addressed to Hibernian FC Competition 2016, Grange Communications Ltd, 22 Great King Street, Edinburgh, EH3 6QH. Entrants must provide their full name, age, address and a daytime telephone number in order to make a valid entry.

6. The Competition will close at 12:00 GMT on Friday 25th March 2016 (the "Closing Date") and any entries received after the Closing Date will not be entered into the Competition. The Competition judging and decision will take place as soon as reasonably practicable following the Closing Date.

### PRIZE

7. Subject to paragraph 8, the prize will consist of one Meet and Greet experience (the "Prize"). If the winner (the "Winner") of the Prize is aged under 18, they must be accompanied by adult to receive their Prize.

8. Grange Communications Ltd reserves the right to substitute the Prize with another of a similar nature at any time.

9. The Prize is non-transferable and there is no cash alternative.

### WINNER

10. The Winner will be selected by an independent judge from all valid entries received on or before the Closing Date.

11. Only the Winner of the Competition will receive notification from Grange Communications Ltd. The Winner will be notified by email or telephone as soon as practicable after the Closing Date. Following the Closing Date, the Winner will be contacted to arrange a mutually convenient date and time to receive their Prize.

# NEW RECRUITS

## JAMES KEATINGS

The signing of striker James Keatings during the summer was all about adding goals and cutting-edge to the team.

Former Scotland Under-19 internationalist James, signed on a two-year contract in June, was originally on the books at Celtic. A move to Hamilton saw him win promotion into the Premiership and he then moved to Tynecastle where he helped Heart of Midlothian win the Championship title – gaining promotion to the top flight in successive seasons. Here's hoping for a Keatings title hat-trick!

One of the players who caught the eye of Head Coach Alan Stubbs in the Championship last season was wide man Dan Carmichael.

He joined Hibernian in the summer after agreeing a two-year contract, following five seasons at Palmerston Park with Queen of the South. Skilful and creative, Daniel will supply width and goal assists at Easter Road.

# NEW RECRUITS

## MARTIN BOYLE

After a successful loan spell, Martin Boyle joined Hibernian on a two-year contract in the summer, following an earlier spell at Easter Road on loan from Dundee.

Originally with Montrose, Boyle joined Dundee in August 2012 and helped the club to win promotion into the Scottish Premiership. He enjoyed a nerve-jangling, but exciting, start to his Hibernian career, making his debut in the Edinburgh Derby at Tynecastle in January 2015.

## MARVIN BARTLEY

Experienced midfielder Marvin Bartley joined Hibernian in the summer on a two-year contract.

He has enjoyed spells with Bournemouth, Burnley and Leyton Orient.

On signing, he said, "I've completely bought into Alan Stubbs' vision for the Club and I'm looking forward to playing my part in his plans to drive the Club forward and earn promotion.

"This is the next chapter in my career and I will be aiming to use the experience I've got to help the team and to make sure it's a season to remember."

The Reading-born 29-year-old stands an impressive 6ft 3ins tall.

## ANTONIO REGUERO

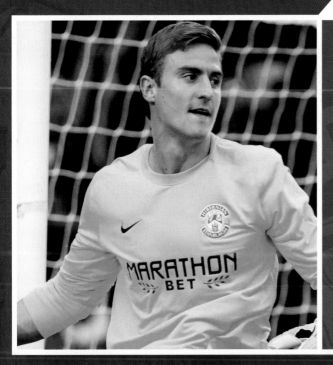

Experienced goalkeeper Antonio Reguero joined Hibernian after spells at Ross County, Kilmarnock and Inverness Caledonian Thistle – so it is fair to say the Spaniard is no stranger to Scottish football.

The 33-year-old was brought on board to provide competition to Mark Oxley.

## DARREN McGREGOR

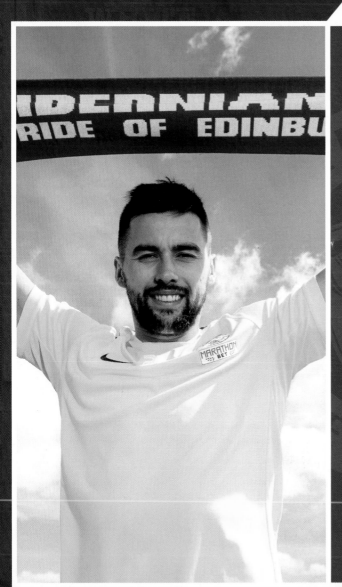

Defender Darren McGregor joined Hibernian on a two-year deal in August.

The player signed up after a successful spell with Rangers. The 30-year-old spent a year at Ibrox and made 53 appearances, earning that club's Player of the Year accolade, but became available in the summer.

The lifelong Hibernian fan was delighted to join his boyhood heroes. "I've supported Hibs my whole life, so to get the opportunity to sign for the club was brilliant.

"I'm really excited about the next chapter of my career at my Club and helping Hibs to challenge for promotion."

McGregor, who can play in central defence or at right-back, was at Cowdenbeath and St Mirren before his move to Rangers.

"He is a strong, experienced player and a good professional," said Easter Road Head Coach Alan Stubbs.

# Quick Quiz

1. Which Hibernian Manager's team were known as the "Tornadoes"?
2. Fraser Fyvie joined Hibernian after a spell at which English club?
3. Which two English sides did Alan Stubbs skipper?
4. In which year did Hibernian last win the League Cup?
5. Name the former Hibernian goalkeeper capped by Scotland at cricket and football?
6. Which French team did Franck Sauzee win the European Cup with?
7. Name the former Hibernian star who was appointed St Mirren Manager at the start of this season?
8. Which was the last stand to be re-built at Easter Road Stadium, completing the ground's redevelopment?
9. Name the first-ever Captain of Hibernian?
10. In which year was the Club founded?
11. Which Hibernian hosts a cult quiz show on Hibernian TV?
12. Who was the Hibernian player who topped the Championship scoring charts last season?
13. Which player celebrates a decade at the Club this season?
14. From which club did Martin Boyle sign?
15. Goalkeeper Mark Oxley was capped for which country at two age levels?
16. Which player was the first signing of Head Coach Alan Stubbs at Hibernian FC?
17. Which African country does Dominique Malonga represent at international level?
18. Where was Moroccan player Farid El Alagui born?

# NEW RECRUITS

Estonian international Henri Anier joined the Club on a loan deal in the summer, to run until the end of the season.

The 24-year-old joined from Dundee United. He is a powerful centre forward who brings others in to play and compliment the qualities of our other strikers.

Head Coach Alan Stubbs said: "We now have strong competition for places within the team and that will bring out the best in the players that are already here."

## ISLAM FERUZ

Striker Islam Feruz joined the Club on a season long loan from English Premier League champions Chelsea in the summer.

Islam, who is 20, has played for Scotland at several youth levels, including U-19, U-20 and U-21. He made his first team debut for Chelsea in July 2013 against a Malaysia League XI in a pre-season match.

Islam said on signing: "I am excited to be back in Scotland and to get some first team football under my belt.

"Hibs have a good young team and I've played with a number of the boys before with the national team.

"The manager has shown faith me and I'm looking forward to repaying it by giving 100%."

Head Coach Alan Stubbs said: "Islam is another really exciting young talent, a player who has fantastic ability and potential, who adds a different dimension to our attacking options."

# ALWAYS BELIEVE IN JONES

He was the inspirational Skipper who scored the opening goal in a famous Cup win, standing tall – all 6ft 7ins of him – to lift the League Cup in front of 30,000 Hibernian supporters before taking a lap of honour to the strains of a spine-tingling rendition of "Sunshine on Leith."

Rob Jones wrote himself into the legend section of Hibernian history by becoming part of a very small club of skippers who have lifted silverware at Hampden when he led the side that scored a stunning 5-1 win over Kilmarnock.

It was the highlight of a happy period at Hibernian for defender Rob, which saw him play most of his football with the exhilarating team led by Manager Tony Mowbray and included the "golden generation" who had come through the Club's Academy system – although the Cup win was achieved under the tenure of John Collins.

Rob played more than 100 games for Hibernian, a period he still remembers fondly.

In a recent interview, Rob – who hails from the North of England and signed for the Club from Grimsby Town – said: "My time at Hibs was a special period in my life. They put me on the map in football terms."

Rob played in a side that included a number of players who had come through the youth system, including goalkeeper Andy McNeil, Kevin Thomson, Scott Brown, Steven Whittaker, Steven Fletcher, and one youngster by the name of Lewis Stevenson, along with other young players brought to the Club by Mowbray including David Murphy, Ivan Sproule and Abdessalam Benjelloun. Many of the players featured in a dream team selection made by Rob some years later, of players he had played with and against. Other stars featured included Messi and Thierry Henry, so starry company indeed!

Most of the players were to feature in the game Rob still defines as the biggest of his career, the final at Hampden where he opened the scoring in the snow en route to the most memorable of days. He said: "It was the biggest game I'd ever played in and that remains the case today – it was fantastic. Being captain of the side and then scoring the first goal in a 5-1 win in a cup final, it doesn't get much better than that. I don't think anyone could have expected the game to go any better, although we could probably have expected the weather to be better because it snowed pretty much all game."

After the final whistle went, the army of Hibernian fans were in unbelievable voice as they sang the Club anthem and moved John Collins and many of the players and others to tears. The memories go on for Rob: "The bus journey went by so quickly on the way back from Glasgow but all the boys were in full voice, as you would expect. Then we went on the open-top bus down to the ground, and the amount of people out on the streets that night to thank us was just fantastic. It was incredible to see how much the result affected so many people. The night seemed to go in a blur but it was the type of occasion that never leaves you."

In his three years at Easter Road Rob played 118 games, scoring twelve goals and joining a small band of fans' favourites, including Jimmy O'Rourke, Mickey Weir and Keith Wright, who all had the distinction of having their own song. Rob's was 'Always believe in Rob Jones: he's indestructible,' to the tune of Spandau Ballet's 'Gold'.

An understandable desire to return to England meant that Rob sparked interest from a number of clubs with a year left on his contract, and he eventually signed for Scunthorpe United for an undisclosed "club record" fee, and left with the best wishes of everyone at Easter Road.

# HIBERNIAN IN THE COMMUNITY

## LEARN TO PLAY THE HIBERNIAN WAY!

Hibernian Community Foundation is committed to helping more people benefit from participation in sport. And for football fans young and old, why not get involved in our football programmes, there's something for everyone.

For more information on all of the courses and programmes, call us on **0131 656 7062** or email us at: **football@hiberniancommunityfoundation.org.uk**

## HIBEE TOTS

Our Hibee Tots programme allows boys and girls to play football from the ages of 2-4. Hibee Tots improves balance, co-ordination, communication, listening skills and confidence using a mixture of activities such as skipping, hopping, running, jumping and fun football-related activities. Our weekly sessions are indoors and delivered by experienced and fully qualified SFA coaches.

Courses run in 8-week blocks.

## FOOTBALL CENTRES

Our Football Centres offer structured sessions for 5-15 year olds, boys and girls. Each week players have the opportunity to take part in fun, challenging activities that will help them to become more skilful, confident and athletic.

Our weekly sessions are delivered by experienced and fully qualified SFA coaches.

Football Centres run in eight-week blocks through the entire football season. All sessions follow a structured curriculum designed to develop individual player's fundamental movement skills.

## HOLIDAY CAMPS

Week-long camps are offered during Easter, Summer, October and February school holidays, for 4-15 year olds, at various locations. Structured coaching sessions offer lots of fun challenges and games, with guest appearances by Hibernian 1st Team players (subject to season).

## DISABILITY FOOTBALL

Football is a fantastic sport, and we believe everyone should have the opportunity to play and to enjoy it. As part of our Disability Football programme, we have strong partnerships with key organisations.

Lothian Hibernian was created in 2008 as a unique partnership with Lothian Special Olympics to provide opportunities for young people with learning disabilities to participate in sport as part of the Hibernian family. As many as 60 people with learning disabilities receive coaching on a regular basis from LSO with assistance from Hibernian Community Foundation.

Working in partnership with the National Deaf Children's Society we are developing a pathway of support for young people who are deaf, including regular, weekly sessions which are also open to hearing friends and siblings. The sessions offer boys and girls from Primary 1 to S2 who are deaf the chance to build their football and interpersonal skills and make new friends.

The Foundation has joined forces with Lothian Autistic Society to offer boys and girls with autism the chance to build their football and interpersonal skills and to make new friends. Regular weekly sessions offer a pathway of support for young people with autism, aged 5-14 from across the Lothians.

## ALAN STUBBS

Head Coach Alan Stubbs is determined that Hibernian supporters will enjoy winning, vibrant and attacking football and is developing a squad of talented players to deliver for supporters.

## MARK OXLEY

One of these was the imposing figure of goalkeeper Mark Oxley. The 6ft 3in stopper signed a two-year deal in the summer after a season-long loan deal from English Premier League club Hull City came to an end. Mark, who began his career with Rotherham United before moving to Humberside, also experienced loan spells with Walsall, Burton Albion and Oldham Athletic. He has been capped by England at both U-18 and U-20 level, but for Hibernian fans his starring moment came on his Scottish Championship debut when he scored a remarkable goal - his goal-kick sailed into the back of Livingston's net at Easter Road in August 2014.

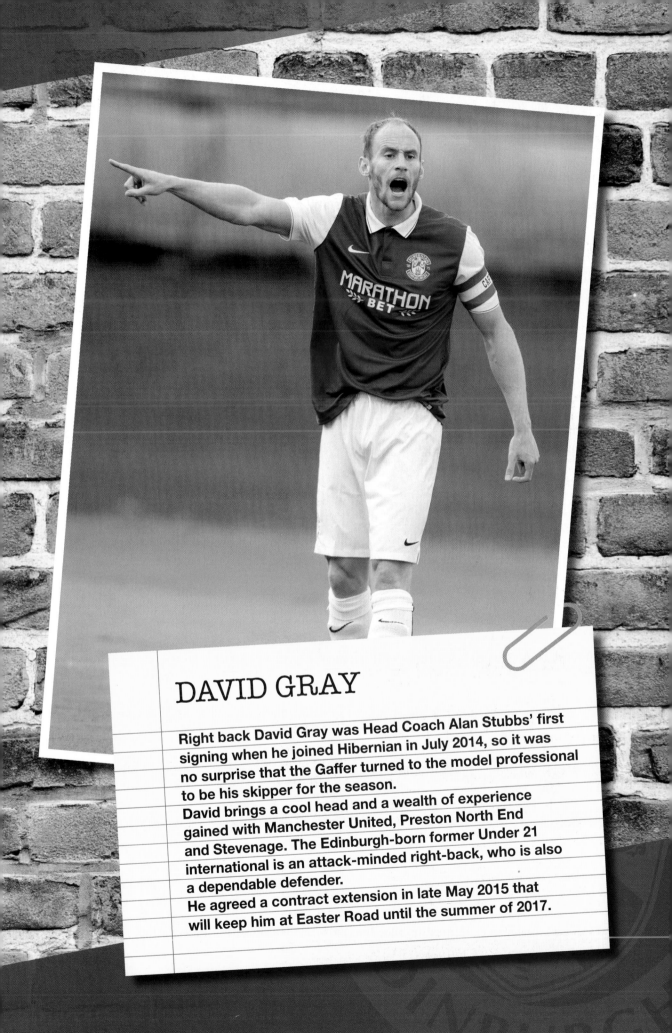

# DAVID GRAY

**Right back David Gray was Head Coach Alan Stubbs' first signing when he joined Hibernian in July 2014, so it was no surprise that the Gaffer turned to the model professional to be his skipper for the season.**

**David brings a cool head and a wealth of experience gained with Manchester United, Preston North End and Stevenage. The Edinburgh-born former Under 21 international is an attack-minded right-back, who is also a dependable defender.**

**He agreed a contract extension in late May 2015 that will keep him at Easter Road until the summer of 2017.**

## PAUL HANLON

Like goalie Mark Oxley, Paul Hanlon has been capped – for Scotland – at two age levels, U-19 and U-21. He also captained the U-21 side.

A product of the Hibernian Academy, Edinburgh-born Paul is a Hibernian fan. He started his first team career at left-back, but has successfully moved into his preferred central defensive role.

He was Hibernian's Player of the Year for both the 2010/2011 and 2013/14 campaigns, and has now made more than 200 appearances for the Club, passing the milestone against Rangers in September 2014.

# LIAM FONTAINE

His partner at the heart of the defence is the experienced Liam Fontaine, who was another to pledge his future to the Club when he signed a two-year contract in the summer. He initally joined Hibernian in the summer of 2014 after an eight-year spell with Bristol City.

His wealth of experience at English Championship level – he was also formerly with Fulham, and had loan spells with Kilmarnock and Yeovil Town – has made him a solid and calm performer. He has been capped at U-20 level by England.

Off the pitch he has become something of a cult figure, presenting a popular and fun quiz show, "Fontaine of Knowledge" on Hibernian TV.

# JORDON FORSTER

Defender Jordon Forster features regularly in first team action, where he has played at both centre-back and full-back.

He joined Hibernian's Academy from Celtic in the summer of 2010 after experiencing loan spells with Berwick Rangers and East Fife.

He made his first team debut in the 2012/13 season in an Edinburgh Derby and produced an assured display at the back to ensure Hibernian won at Tynecastle.

## LEWIS STEVENSON

The Club's longest-serving player, Kirkcaldy-born Lewis Stevenson, hits a remarkable milestone this season when he chalks up his tenth season at the Club – unusual in the modern game.

Lewis first hit the headlines in 2007, when as a teenager he was named man of the match after Hibernian's CIS Cup triumph. He agreed to extend his stay at the Club still further when he signed a new deal this summer.

He plays either in midfield or in defence, at left-back, and has already chalked up over 200 first team appearances – like Paul Hanlon reaching the career milestone last season. He also scored a goal of the season contender in a 2-0 win over Rangers at Ibrox.

## FRASER FYVIE

Midfielder Fraser Fyvie delighted Alan Stubbs and supporters in the summer when he agreed a new two-year contract.

Fraser originally joined the club in February on a short term deal, and was widely expected to be likely to move on. But the former Scotland U-21 internationalist decided he enjoyed the brand of football being played at Easter Road, and committed to a new deal.

Fraser spent two and a half years with Wigan Athletic before joining Hibernian. He first came through the ranks with Aberdeen.

## LIAM HENDERSON

Liam Henderson joined the Club for the season in August. The talented midfielder arrived at Easter Road on a one-year loan deal from Celtic, where he recently signed a new three-year contract.

Alan Stubbs, said: "Liam is one of the best and most talented young players in Scotland. He's a good, modern midfielder who can score goals, and he has played first team football for both Celtic and Rosenborg. He's an exciting player I rate really highly and I am delighted that he has joined us."

## SCOTT MARTIN

Head Coach Alan Stubbs is hopeful that midfielder Scott Martin's continued development will see him play a greater first team role this season. A Scotland U-19 internationalist, Martin made his senior debut as a substitute against Falkirk in December of last year. Born in Glasgow, he has progressed through the Club's Academy system.

## SAM STANTON

Another Academy graduate, Sam Stanton, has already made a significant impact at first team level with the Club he has supported all his life. A Leither, Sam is no relation to all-time great and former captain Pat, and has progressed up through the youth ranks at Easter Road before making his first team debut during the 2011/12 season.

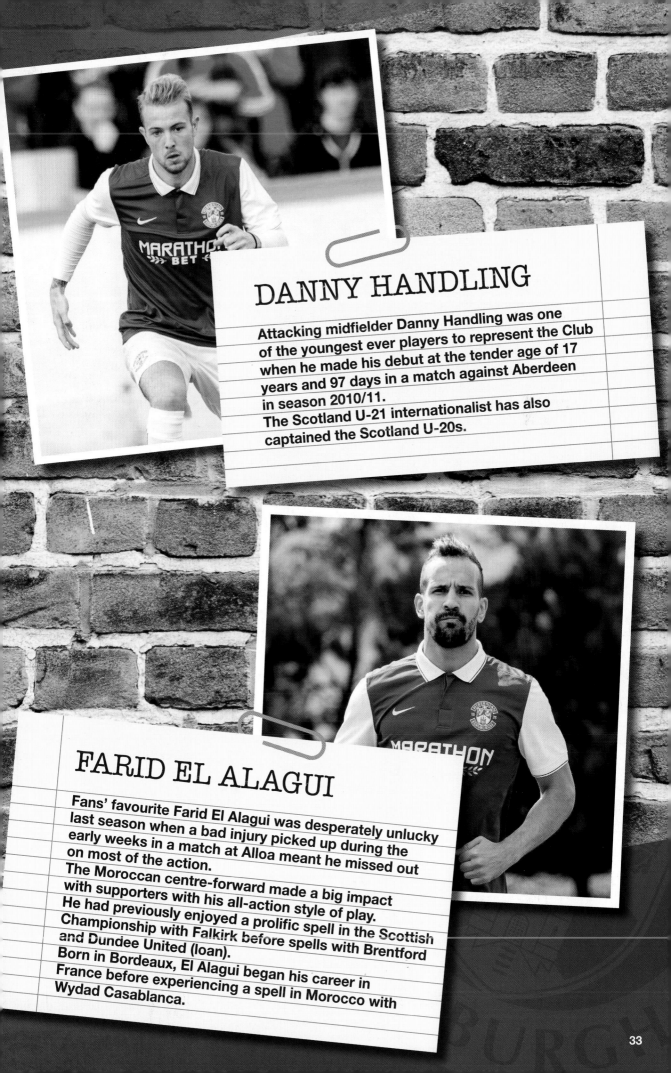

## DANNY HANDLING

Attacking midfielder Danny Handling was one of the youngest ever players to represent the Club when he made his debut at the tender age of 17 years and 97 days in a match against Aberdeen in season 2010/11.
The Scotland U-21 internationalist has also captained the Scotland U-20s.

## FARID EL ALAGUI

Fans' favourite Farid El Alagui was desperately unlucky last season when a bad injury picked up during the early weeks in a match at Alloa meant he missed out on most of the action.
The Moroccan centre-forward made a big impact with supporters with his all-action style of play.
He had previously enjoyed a prolific spell in the Scottish Championship with Falkirk before spells with Brentford and Dundee United (loan).
Born in Bordeaux, El Alagui began his career in France before experiencing a spell in Morocco with Wydad Casablanca.

## JASON CUMMINGS

Jason Cummings finished last season as the leading scorer in the Scottish Championship.

A striker in the "cheeky" mould, Jason's knack for scoring important goals and his colourful post-match interviews have made him one of the league's personalities.

The striker joined Hibernian's Academy from Hutchison Vale in the summer of 2013, and he quickly made an impact at U-20 level and pushed himself into first team contention.

He made his debut as a substitute against Inverness in November 2013.

# DOMINIQUE MALONGA

Striker Dominique Malonga enjoyed a solid, prolific start to his spell in Scottish football when he joined Hibernian last summer – but the experienced player will be hoping for even better this season.

Dominique is a player with real pedigree, being capped by France at U-19 level, before subsequently deciding to play for Congo, whom he represented last season in the African Cup of Nations. He has also played in France, Italy and Spain, after coming through the vaunted Academy at FC Monaco.

He moved from France to Torino before a loan spell with Foggia. He won the Serie B title with Cesena and has also been out on loan to Real Murcia in Spain.

# LEWIS ALLAN

Young striker Lewis Allan spent last season on loan at Dunfermline to gain vital experience, with big things expected of the young Borderer.

# EASTER ROAD
# RECORD
# ATTENDANCE

The opening of the East Stand at Easter Road in 2010 completed the redevelopment of the ground and increased the capacity to just over 20,000.

However, the record attendance that took place at the stadium 65 years ago – in the days before all-seater stadia – dwarfed that figure.

At that time the huge post-war-crowds that were attending games at Easter Road made it imperative that the capacity of the ground be increased, and work had been ongoing behind the main terracing for several months to extend the maximum to just under 70,000, a rise of almost 10,000.

Both Hibs and Hearts had shown a rich vein of form on the run up to the traditional New Year's Day derby on 2 January 1950, and a tremendous sense of anticipation and excitement had been building in the city for several weeks.

On the day of the game sizable queues had started to form well before the gates opened at midday for the 2.15 kick off, and such was the demand that the gates had to be closed 15 minutes before the start with thousands still locked outside desperately trying to gain admission. Meanwhile several dozen already inside the ground made their way to the exits after finding it impossible to even see the pitch because of the thronging crowds.

At one stage the crowds had stretched four or five deep along both sides of Albion Road, up Easter Road as far as Rossie Place and down as far as Dalmeny Street, with similar scenes at both St Clair Street and Hawkhill.

Mounted police were called in to try to maintain order and they struggled to contain the masses both inside and outside the ground while the volunteer ambulance men were kept busy dealing with dozens of casualties on the pitch. The ambulance men also found themselves overworked transporting the thankfully mainly minor injury victims to the makeshift casualty station inside the adjacent Albion Road School, although several people were later taken to hospital. It is reported that two people died due to the effects of the crushing, one at the game itself, the other soon after arriving home from the game.

The game eventually got underway with hundreds of spectators lining the trackside, threatening on occasion to spill over on to the playing surface.

In the opening forty five minutes Hibs were well on top as Hearts were forced to withstand severe pressure, goalkeeper Brown in outstanding form. Midway through the half Hibs took the lead when a Willie Ormond cross from the left wing found the inrushing Gordon Smith perfectly placed to bullet a header past the Hearts goalkeeper and that was the score at the interval. In the second half however it was a different story as Hearts scored twice to take the lead, but in the closing stages only several magnificent saves by Brown denied the home side a deserved share of the points.

1

HAIR:
EYES:
CHIN:

2

HAIR:
EYES:
CHIN:

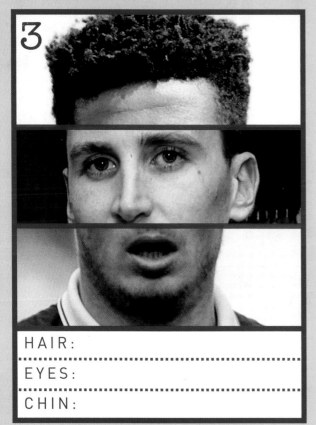

3

HAIR:
EYES:
CHIN:

# In Disguise

We've mixed up a few Hibernians' head shots to make some weird and wonderful faces.

Can you tell whose hair, eyes and chins are pictured?

ANSWERS ON p60

# DNIPRO 10 YEARS ON

In September 2005 Hibernian travelled to Dnipropetrovsk in the Ukraine for a UEFA Cup match against FC Dnipro – last season's runners up in the same competition, now renamed the Europa League.

The two sides had fought out a nil each draw at Easter Road, and Tony Mowbray's talented and exciting young team travelled hopefully to the Ukraine. A 5-1 defeat was unkind on the visitors, but there was no denying that the better side on the night was victorious.

Hibernian fans travelled in numbers, as ever, and a group of fans visited a local orphanage to take gifts and, moved by the conditions they encountered, set about raising funds. Within a few months the idea snowballed and the well-meaning Hibernian support had an official charity to its name – Dnipro Kids. Ten years on and the charity is still going strong, with Steven Carr still at the Chair and he and his committee working as hard as ever to raise funds.

The charity now employs people in the Ukraine, and has continued to support children throughout their time in orphanages, in foster homes, and even through the ongoing conflict.

The story is one of which everyone at Hibernian is extremely proud. If you want to help, visit the website at dniprokids.com.

Ally MacLeod

George Best

John Burridge

# Hibernian Mavericks

They're the great entertainers, the guys with big talent and – often – big attitudes to match. They're the footballing mavericks, and often they are the players that supporters take to their hearts.

Hibernian has enjoyed its fair share of footballing genius – often flawed genius - over the years, and fans cherish the memories that these unorthodox players provide.

George Best, John "Budgie" Burridge, Russell Latapy, Ally MacLeod, and Chic Charnley are a handful that spring to mind, the men who could turn a game in a flash of inspiration. Or they could equally make headlines for antics that had little to do with gathering points.

However they made the news, they were players supporters enjoyed going to Easter Road to watch and in this year's annual we are happy to pay tribute to our own clutch of Mavericks.

Ally MacLeod was an inspiration signing when he joined from Southampton in 1974. He was to finish

top scorer in all competitions for the Club in each of the seasons 76/77 to 80/81, scoring 99 goals.

Talented, elegant, he was capable of the kind of brilliance that wins matches with breathtaking ease. In one encounter with Dundee in front of television cameras, he stroked a superb free kick into the net only to have the goal disallowed and ordered to be re-taken. Undeterred, MacLeod perfectly replicated the first strike.

Much was expected of his link-up with George Best when the mercurial Irishman joined Hibernian in 1979 in an ultimately failed attempt to stave off relegation.

Best's arrival put thousands on gates all over Scotland, and he brought flair and colour, if not reliability, to his short spell in the Scottish game. His alcohol issues were never far from the surface, but he remained hugely popular with supporters – on one occasion jokingly motioning to drink from a can thrown at him at Ibrox by a Rangers fan.

Chic Charnley

Russell Latapy

"Budgie" was a goalkeeper who personified the tradition the goalies are a bit different. He played for almost 30 clubs in a career that spanned three decades, playing almost 800 top-flight games including 77 at Hibernian in the early 1990s, making his debut for the club at almost 40-years-old!

A League Cup winner, the extrovert Burridge exuded confidence that rubbed off on team-mates and fans alike, but he was equally loved for his eccentric antics including his own pre-match warm-up and his penchant for perching on the crossbar.

Russell Latapy, the "little magician" from Trinidad and Tobago, brought verve and flair to an excellent Hibernian side put together by Alex McLeish, the cornerstone of which came to be the link-up play of Latapy and "Le God", Franck Sauzee.

Russell was extravagantly talented and could win matches with a swing of his hips or a flash of brilliance, but he was equally likely to receive a hard stare from his Manager for off-field antics

that saw him give full reign to his zest for la dolce vita. He was a magical player though, and his sheer talent meant he earned his place as a maverick that fans adored.

Chic Charnley was viewed as a talented but journeyman player when he signed for Hibernian in the summer of 1997. He made his debut against his beloved Celtic at Easter Road that August, latching on to the misplaced pass of a Celtic debutant, one Henrik Larsson, to smash in an unstoppable 25-yarder.

A tough and humorous Glaswegian Charnley, who once famously disarmed a teenage tearaway carrying a samurai sword despite being wounded in the hand by the blade, enjoyed the best form of his career at Hibernian.

# SPOT THE BALL

## Can you work out which is the real ball in the picture below?

ANSWERS ON p60

# HiBS KiDS

Hibs Kids launched for 2015/16 with an incredible package available for wee Hibees aged 11 and under.

Hibs Kids members all receive a host of benefits including a membership card, season planner and certificate on joining, as well as a birthday card from the Club and a pantomime (0-8 year olds) or football festival (9-11 year olds) at Christmas.

Child season ticket holders are automatically Hibs Kids. Hibs Kids members who don't have a season ticket will be able to receive five free tickets for Hibs Kids games, and season ticket

holders will also be able to bring a 0-17 year old to Hibs Kids games for only £5! The Hibs Kids matches remaining for this season are:

**Saturday 12 March: Hibernian v Livingston**

**Saturday 16 April: Hibernian v Falkirk**

**Saturday 29 August: Hibernian v Raith Rovers**

Hibs Kids have already enjoyed three matches at Easter Road, against Raith Rovers, Dumbarton and Queen of the South.

All Hibs Kids are also entered into a free draw to lead the team out as a matchday mascot or take part in the Hibs Kids half time challenge.

All this for only £15 per membership! To buy your wee Hibee's membership visit the Hibernian eTicketing website, visit the Ticket Office (open Monday-Friday 10am-5pm, Saturday 10am-3pm) or call 0844 844 1875.

HiBS KiDS
Sign up now for 2015-16

Sunshine
The Leith Lynx

# FRASER FYVIE

## MIDFIELDER

The signing of a new two-year deal by midfielder Fraser Fyvie was greeted with huge pleasure by Hibernian supporters this summer.

The talented and exciting player – still in his early 20s – has excited supporters happy to see Head Coach Alan Stubbs continue with his quest of bringing skilful footballers with much to prove to the Club.

Fraser was a stand-out performer last season after joining Hibernian on a six-month loan deal. And it was the direction of travel that Alan Stubbs wants to take the Club that persuaded him to stay on. Fraser said: "Moving back up to Scotland has been really beneficial to my career, the manager gave me a platform to play games and I wanted to repay him by committing my future to the Club for the next two years.

"This was an easy and exciting decision to make.

"I think we just missed out last season; everyone came away from it disappointed, but I'm confident that we can take the extra step and go up.

"Everyone within the squad believes we've started to build something special here at the club and now we want to kick on and achieve success."

Fraser first came to prominence at Aberdeen where he played more than 50 times before signing for Wigan in July 2012. Loan spells at Yeovil and Shrewsbury preceded a move to Leith on a short-term deal.

He set a number of records when he first broke into the senior ranks in Aberdeen, becoming the youngest ever player to play for the reds when he made his debut against Hamilton Academical at the age of 16, and won the Man of the Match award for the game.

Pleasingly for Hibernian fans, he scored his first senior goal for Aberdeen on 27 January 2010, against Hearts at Tynecastle. This goal made him the youngest ever goalscorer in a Scottish Premier League match, breaking the record previously held by Dundee United player David Goodwillie

# LIAM FONTAINE

## DEFENDER

Liam Fontaine has proven to be one of Head Coach Alan Stubbs' most astute signings – with the big defender playing a key role in the team's improved performances.

The centre-half has big experience gained in his time in England with Fulham and Bristol City in particular, where he played many games in the English Championship, and he has been capped at several youth levels by England.

It was widely expected that Liam would return to England, in all probability to play in the Championship, but he elected to re-sign on a new two-year contract at Hibernian.

At the time, he said: "I really enjoyed last season and now the aim is to add to the progress that we made and go one step further by getting up to the Premiership.

"We didn't win the play-offs, which was obviously disappointing. But you use that and hopefully we can learn from it.

"We need to be consistent and see games out a bit better. There were games we dominated and didn't get the result. I think that's the one thing we need to change this year."

He's proven to be a popular player off-the-field as well as on it, one of the leaders in the team dressing room. In addition, he presents a fun magazine show on Hibernian TV called "Fontaine of Knowledge". Liam has struck up a solid and stylish central defensive partnership with Paul Hanlon, making 38 appearances last season.

Yet it was at the other end of the pitch where Fontaine once again made headlines when he netted in a game for Bristol City against Wolves.

Then Bristol City boss Gary Johnson had offered to moon in a menswear store window in Bristol if Fontaine scored – and when the defender did the potential caused some hilarity.

Liam remembered: "Gary said he'd do it if I scored but in the end he wasn't allowed to for health and safety reasons.

"But it was a good incentive. Alan Stubbs doesn't have to offer a similar incentive for me to score...yet. I got two last season, but my goal scoring isn't the best."

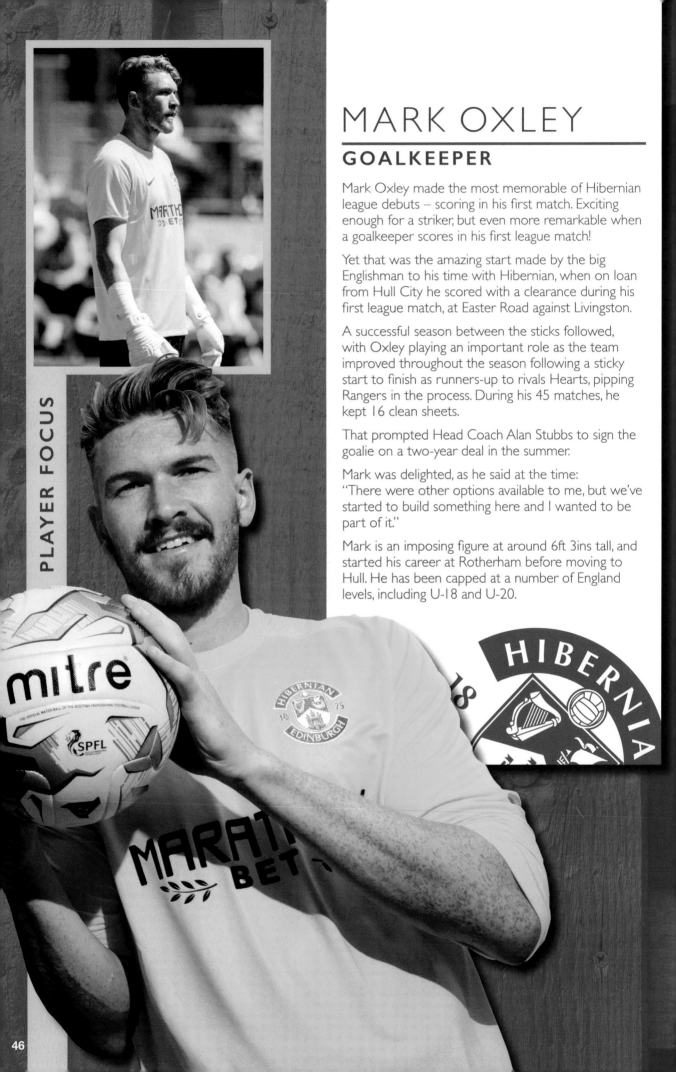

# MARK OXLEY

## GOALKEEPER

Mark Oxley made the most memorable of Hibernian league debuts – scoring in his first match. Exciting enough for a striker, but even more remarkable when a goalkeeper scores in his first league match!

Yet that was the amazing start made by the big Englishman to his time with Hibernian, when on loan from Hull City he scored with a clearance during his first league match, at Easter Road against Livingston.

A successful season between the sticks followed, with Oxley playing an important role as the team improved throughout the season following a sticky start to finish as runners-up to rivals Hearts, pipping Rangers in the process. During his 45 matches, he kept 16 clean sheets.

That prompted Head Coach Alan Stubbs to sign the goalie on a two-year deal in the summer.

Mark was delighted, as he said at the time: "There were other options available to me, but we've started to build something here and I wanted to be part of it."

Mark is an imposing figure at around 6ft 3ins tall, and started his career at Rotherham before moving to Hull. He has been capped at a number of England levels, including U-18 and U-20.

# DAVID GRAY

## DEFENDER

The Club Captain was the first player Head Coach Alan Stubbs brought in when he came to Hibernian, and the full-back has been a key man ever since.

A graduate of the Heart of Midlothian youth system, Gray's potential was spotted early and won him a move to English giants Manchester United as a teenager, with Hearts receiving a fee for the then youth player.

The right-back spent six years at United, making a first team appearance during a League Cup match, and also spent four seasons out on loan to English sides Plymouth and Crewe Alexandra, as well as in Belgium to Royal Antwerp. He was signed by Preston North End after his time at United, and also played for Burton Albion and Stevenage before joining Hibernian.

Tough, pacy, strong in the tackle and a ready attacker, David is the epitome of the modern full-back and his strong performances and presence in the dressing room prompted the Gaffer to make him his skipper this season.

The 27-year-old then extended his own deal with Hibernian, and was delighted when the Head Coach and his staff did likewise.

The Captain said: "He's been great for me, and he was a driving force for a lot of the players because of the environment he has created."

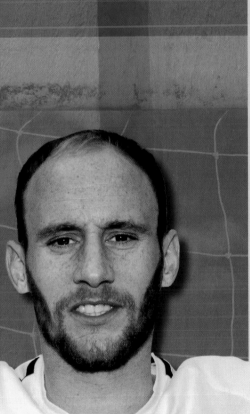

PLAYER FOCUS

# 10 Facts About...

## JORDON FORSTER

1.  Jordon joined Hibernian from Celtic in 2010.

2.  He can play centre-back or right-back.

3.  Jordon stands 6ft 2in tall.

4.  He has also played on loan at Berwick Rangers.

5.  Jordon has played almost 50 times for the first team.

6.  He made his debut in 2013, in a 2-1 win against Hearts.

7.  He has scored five goals.

8.  Jordon originally hails from Gorgie.

9.  He attended the same school, Boroughmuir, as Hibs legend Lawrie Reilly.

10. His nickname is Fozzy.

MARK OXLEY

# ONES TO WATCH

Two young full-backs will be hoping to force their way into Head Coach Alan Stubbs' thinking during the course of this season.

Callum Crane and Aaron Dunsmore will be hoping for a breakthrough season in terms of competitive first team involvement.

The two youngsters, both born in Edinburgh, are regarded as good prospects.

In March of 2015 Development squad player Dunsmore extended his contract with Hibs until 2017. The teenage right-back has been a regular for Joe McBride's U-20 side in the SPFL Development League and has also made the bench for the first team. The lifelong Hibs fan, from Musselburgh, said:

"To be able to play for the team I've always supported is a dream come true. Hopefully now I can continue working towards making the step up into playing for the first team."

Left-back Crane also extended his contract, in January 2015, until 2018. The 19-year-old said he was delighted at the news, and said: "My objective is to now continue developing and break into the first team." Development Coach Joe McBride expressed his pleasure at both contracts, adding: "This is the next stage in the journey for both of them, and I look forward to them continuing to develop at Hibernian."

Head Coach Alan Stubbs said: "There is a clear pathway through from the Academy to the first team squad and the incentives are there for players to seize their opportunities.

"As a club, it is important that we develop young players, who then commit for the long-term benefit and future of Hibernian."

AARON DUNSMORE

CALLUM CRANE

# BIG new fan...

## WHITNEY MERCILUS

Hibernian attracted a new – and large – celebrity fan in the considerable shape of American Footballer Whitney Mercilus.

A star linebacker with the Houston Texans, Whitney used a holiday in Scotland to indulge his passion for "soccer" by adopting Hibernian as his team, attending a match as a guest of the Club and spending a day with the squad at the Hibernian Training Centre.

The highly-rated 24-year-old, 19-stone colossus has become a fully-fledged Hibee and he was handed a full Hibernian kit by Head Coach Alan Stubbs complete with 'Mercilus, 59' on the back.

Mercilus also met players including American Football fans goalkeeper Mark Oxley and centre-half Liam Fontaine at the Training Centre.

He said: "I'm a huge football fan and Hibs are now my favourite team.

"I'm already planning to come back over next year and I'm looking forward to going to another game at Easter Road – the atmosphere at Sunday's game was awesome."

# NEW RECRUIT

## DYLAN McGEOUCH

Head Coach Alan Stubbs finally got his man in August when Dylan McGeouch signed for Hibernian on a three-year deal. The talented midfielder joined the Club from Celtic for an undisclosed fee.

Dylan had enjoyed a successful loan spell with Hibernian the previous season, and Alan Stubbs saw him as central to his plans going forward.

Alan said: "It's no secret that I am a great admirer of Dylan as a player. He was really important to us when he was here on loan last season, and I've been trying to get him back here ever since.

"I'm delighted we managed to get him, even though it took a bit of time. He is an important player for us this season and in the seasons to come."

Dylan said: "I am very happy to be back at Hibernian. I enjoy working with the Gaffer and his staff and I enjoy the kind of football we play. The Club is going in the right direction, and it is an exciting time."

The 22-year-old has been capped for Scotland at U-16, 17, 19 and U-21 level. Dylan made his debut for Celtic in 2011, and scored an outstanding goal for the Glasgow club in his second appearance the same year. He also spent time on loan at Coventry City.

# COLOUR ME IN

Defender Liam Fontaine is looking a little peaky. Get out your colouring pencils or pens and bring him back to his full-colour fitness.

# WORDSEARCH

HIBERNIAN CAPTAINS: find the surnames of 12 players who have captained Hibs.

| | | | | | | | | | | | |
|---|---|---|---|---|---|---|---|---|---|---|---|
| J | B | F | Y | K | H | U | N | T | E | R | H |
| B | L | C | A | L | D | W | E | L | L | U | N |
| A | R | A | M | A | N | C | M | T | G | L | N |
| R | X | M | Y | R | Y | C | R | H | M | X | A |
| K | S | L | U | J | L | A | E | W | C | N | H |
| C | A | M | R | R | W | S | N | M | T | O | A |
| V | U | T | A | E | R | K | T | S | T | T | L |
| N | Z | T | T | C | C | A | E | N | R | N | E |
| M | E | S | W | T | L | N | Y | R | P | A | H |
| G | E | L | T | A | O | E | K | J | K | T | W |
| X | X | C | N | J | H | B | O | L | G | S | B |
| F | D | G | Q | Q | R | S | B | D | H | T | C |

Stanton       Sauzee        Whelahan

Jones         Hughes        Stewart

Hunter        McNamara      Caldwell

MacLeod       Shaw          Murray

Answers on p60

55

# HIBERNIAN
## LADIES & GIRLS

Hibernian Ladies have enjoyed another successful season – with strong league form including an away win against arch rivals Glasgow City.

An excellent League Cup run also saw the Ladies reach the final, only to be denied in a thrilling match by 2-1 by Glasgow City.

The club has operated under the Hibernian banner since 1999 and has become one of the leading clubs for women and girls in Scottish football, with a whole string of titles and trophies under their belt.

The elite Scottish Women's Premier League team is one of the powerhouses in the women's game in Scotland, competing at the top of all competitions with Glasgow City in particular.

But the club is all about participation, and is now an integral part of the Hibernian Community Foundation and its community football programme, with many of its matches and training sessions taking place at the Hibernian Training Centre at East Mains.

Hibernian Girls and Ladies FC offer players of all ages a chance to play the sport with teams at all age groups: U-11s, U-13s, U-15s, U-17s, Development Squad and Premier League.

The growth in the game for women and girls means that the Club are always on the lookout for coaches, first-aiders, match analysts and others, as well as new players. If you are interested in getting involved, more information is available online at:

www.pitchero.com/clubs/hiberniangirlsladiesfc.

Hibernian's Heather Richards (2nd left) celebrates her strike with team-mates.

Glasgow City's Denise O'Sullivan (right) battles with Lisa Robertson for possession.

# HIBERNIAN
## SUPPORTERS LIMITED

It's not just on the pitch that has seen dramatic change and progress over the past year…

The Club's decision to put in place the opportunity for supporters to own up to 51% of the shares – a controlling interest – represented the start of a potential new era.

One group of supporters determined to play their part were the directors of Hibernian Supporters Limited, an organisation established for one purpose only – to raise money from supporters to buy and hold shares in the Club on their behalf.

The well-known Hibernian faces are (from left) Gordon Smith, Kenny MacAskill, Club Chief Executive Leeann Dempster, Charlie Reid, Jim Adie and Stephen Dunn. Missing from this picture was another director, Hibernian legend Jackie McNamara.

Six months in and the group had almost 1000 members, and was targeting to achieve more within its first year, and in the process raised valuable cash to help fund the Club's football ambition. Our second picture shows Gordon Smith handing over a cheque to Club Head Coach Alan Stubbs.

The Club's unique share offer means that all money used to buy shares directly benefits the Club. None of the funds raised benefits any existing shareholder.

Contributing to HSL couldn't be easier, and provides a way for supporters to contribute what they can afford each month to help supporters gain a major say in the running of their club in a way that helps fund football – winners all round. More information is available at:

http://hiberniansupporters.co.uk.

# HIBERNIAN HISTORY & HONOURS

## HISTORY AT A GLANCE

- Founded in 1875 in Edinburgh's "Little Ireland" – the Cowgate.

- The name derives from Latin and means Irishmen.

- Scottish Cup winners in 1887, and a defeat of Preston North End the same year saw Hibernian crowned "World Club Champions".

- Greatest era – The Famous Five years in the 1950s which secured league championships and saw Hibernian as the first British Club to compete in the European Cup, losing at the semi-final stage.

- A second golden era during the 1970s when "Turnbull's Tornadoes" won silverware and played thrilling football.

- Attempted takeover by Hearts owner Wallace Mercer in 1990 as Hibernian faces financial melt-down, leads to the launch of the Hands Off Hibs campaign to save the Club.

- Present owner Sir Tom Farmer CBE saves the Club from extinction, and a League Cup win follows shortly after in 1991.

- Stadium redeveloped in 1990s and at the turn of the decade.

- Hibernian wins League Cup in 5-1 win over Kilmarnock in March 2007.

- Club opens Hibernian Training Centre in December 2007.

- Stadium redevelopment completed with opening of new East Stand, summer 2010.

## HONOURS

| | |
|---|---|
| Scottish League Winners (4) | 1902/03, 1947/48, 1950/51, 1951/52 |
| First Division winners (2) | 1980/81, 1998/99 |
| Division Two winners (3) | 1893/94, 1894/95, 1932/33 |
| Division One runners-up (6) | 1896/97, 1946/47, 1949/50, 1952/53, 1973/74, 1974/75 |
| Scottish Cup winners (2) | 1887, 1902 |
| Scottish Cup runners-up (11) | 1896, 1914, 1923, 1924, 1947, 1958, 1972, 1979, 2001 2012, 2013 |
| Scottish League Cup winners (3) | 1972/73, 1991/92, 2006/07 |
| Scottish League Cup runners-up (6) | 1950/51, 1968/69, 1974/75, 1985/86, 1993/94, 2003/04 |
| Drybrough Cup winners (2) | 1972/73, 1973/74 |
| Summer Cup winners (2) | 1941, 1964 |

## Quick Quiz p20

1. Eddie Turnbull
2. Wigan
3. Bolton and Everton
4. 2007
5. Andy Goram
6. Marseilles
7. Ian Murray
8. East Stand
9. Michael Whelahan
10. 1875
11. Liam Fontaine
12. Jason Cummings
13. Lewis Stevenson
14. Dundee
15. England
16. David Gray
17. Congo
18. France

## In Disguise Quiz p37

1. **Hair:** Martin Boyle
   **Eyes:** John McGinn
   **Chin:** Marvin Bartley

2. **Hair:** David Gray
   **Eyes:** Alan Stubbs
   **Chin:** Liam Fontaine

3. **Hair:** Dominique Malonga
   **Eyes:** Paul Hanlon
   **Chin:** Fraser Fyvie

## Spot the Ball p42

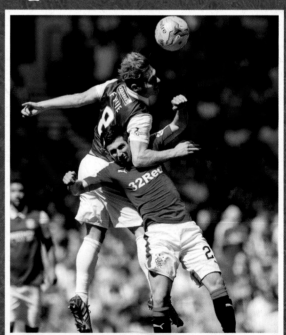

## Wordsearch p55

| J | B | F | Y | K | H | U | N | T | E | R | H |
|---|---|---|---|---|---|---|---|---|---|---|---|
| B | L | C | A | L | D | W | E | L | L | U | N |
| A | R | A | M | A | N | C | M | T | G | L | N |
| R | X | M | Y | R | Y | C | R | H | M | X | A |
| K | S | L | U | J | L | A | E | W | C | N | H |
| C | A | M | R | R | W | S | N | M | T | O | A |
| V | U | T | A | E | R | K | T | S | T | T | L |
| N | Z | T | T | C | C | A | E | N | R | N | E |
| M | E | S | W | T | L | N | Y | R | P | A | H |
| G | E | L | T | A | O | E | K | J | K | T | W |
| X | X | C | N | J | H | B | O | L | G | S | B |
| F | D | G | Q | Q | R | S | B | D | H | T | C |

# CONTACT DETAILS

EMAIL                                           club@hibernianfc.co.uk

TEL                                                   0131 661 2159

WEBSITE                                          www.hibernianfc.co.uk

TWITTER                                                @HibsOfficial

FACEBOOK                                       Hibernian Football Club

YOUTUBE                                                   HibsTV

INSTAGRAM                                                 hibspics


## MEETINGS & EVENTS

email: catering@hibernianfc.co.uk
tel: 0131 656 7075


## CLUB STORE

0131 656 7078


Hibernian Football Club, Easter Road Stadium
12 Albion Place, Edinburgh, EH7 5QG